Wishbone Dance

Wishbone Dance

New & selected medical poems

Glen Downie

Glen Downie

Salt Lake City
October 2000

Wolsak and Wynn . Toronto

Typeset in Times New Roman, printed in Canada by
The Coach House Printing Company, Toronto.

Front cover art: "Puppets" – Munich State Museum; photograph: Glen Downie
Cover design: Stan Bevington
Author's photograph: G. Charles

The publishers gratefully acknowledge the support of the Canada Council for the Arts for our publishing program.

Wolsak and Wynn Publishers Ltd.
Post Office Box 316
Don Mills, Ontario, Canada M3C 2S7

Canadian Cataloguing in Publication Data

Glen Downie-
Wishbone Dance

Poems.
ISBN 0-919897-64-9

I. Title.

PS8557.O82W47 1999   C811'.54   C99-930857-2
PR9199.3.D68W47 1999

ACKNOWLEDGEMENTS

Before these poems took form, I'd already come home stained, skinned, stinking — from packing boxes in the warehouse, digging pools for the wealthy, caring for the disabled. The material world surrounds, presses in, & sometimes discloses its sacred heart. Later there were crisis lines & visits to the dying; then social work school, & a small Catholic hospital. All training aside, I never felt ready for any of it, so I sought out whatever might help me understand. Some folks thought I harboured a secret hope of becoming a doctor. But it wasn't that.

The "Valentine Flasher" poems grew out of work in St. Vincent's Hospital, as the government of the day was imposing a 'restraint program' on health care.. My thanks to everyone there, especially Norman Wignall, Pat Rebbeck, & the late Herc Cserepes, for their generosity during difficult times. The poems of "The Cut Day" arose out of many later years at the A. Maxwell Evans Clinic. Again, thanks to the patients & families, my colleagues in Social Work, & the other staff & volunteers. Special thanks are due Liz Dohan for her practical friendship, & to Ray Allen & Joe Connors, who taught by example. Inspiration for the "Black Thread" poems came from relief work in other settings, from the experiences of friends & colleagues, from personal & family life, & from all those medical images that took no notice of off-hours or holidays.

Thanks to Dale for the source material for 'Information...' & for other kindnesses beyond counting. And to Jock, my gratitude for believing in the continued usefulness of these poems, many of which were first published in books now out of print: *An X-ray of Longing* (Polestar Press), *Heartland* (Mosaic Press) & *The Angel of Irrational Numbers* (Press Porcépic). Of the poems not from the above-mentioned collections, 'Living with Cancer' was published in *More Than Our Jobs* (Pulp Press) & 'Diagnosis: Heart Failure' in *Waves*. Others have recently appeared in, or been accepted by *The Lancet, The Journal of Emergency Medicine, The Journal of Family Practice, Split Shift,* & *Mediphors.* Thanks to the editors of those publications.

PROLOGUE

My first caller on the suicide phone
whispered something I'd never heard of:
colostomy   *Couldn't fake it*
Had to ask her to explain

She said It makes you
socially unacceptable

then she gave up
You wouldn't understand
Left me with an earful
of it's-all-over
dead-line buzz

1. VALENTINE FLASHER

... no longer
young Sunny Jim from the cereal box

Worker Classification: Material Handler

We work in the world you & I handling
coal chandeliers razor blades hamburger
whatever they ask us to carry sort shovel
A box of glass eyes or tear gas cartridges
Mud silk marshmallows guns potatoes
One man handles diamonds another garbage
Chalk or cheese we come home stained
skinned stinking

I've wiped the asses of grown men
You've smashed up old batteries
the splashed acid eats at your jeans
Do we work because we're hungry
for substance? Is it even lonelier
for mathematicians?

Pat cuts off a cancerous breast —
the day's work has begun How does it feel
when a severed breast slips off into your hand?
Catherine dresses up stillborns in the morgue
so parents can say goodbye
The babies are cold & pale as congealed fat
I ask her: *How do you handle a dead baby?*

This is the way the world works: you build a house
as I tear one down We need each other
Hands must be full of something
Who knows how we came to be here
We are groping like the newly blind
for anything familiar
for anything at all

They introduce you to the water
by throwing you
in the deep end

Welcome to the life
Welcome to the work

A near-death experience
soon to be followed
by another
& another
& another...

Diagnosis: Heart Failure

Complaints in all her systems   (*Listen*
to her chest   The fussy old sweet-
heart's congested)   Can you cough up love?
Can you produce anything for us?
Breathless
she gasps for the mask
They want to wean her
from oxygen   *The elderly*
someone says *are like children*
They are forever

nagging her to leave
the bed & totter down halls
Whatever happened to Christian charity? she croaks
In the corridor they've hung gentle Jesus
To her he exposes his
bloodless symmetrical heart
like a Valentine flasher

The doctrine now is restraint
of expectations   Patients are not encouraged
to lean on the staff
who fear dependence
may somehow be infectious
To stem the epidemic
get well or get out   Besides
what nursing home will take her
if she insists on breathing

oxygen   It's a fire
hazard after all   So
she staggers on wheezing
dramatically   They refuse
to be suckered   They harden
their hearts *for her own good*
deny her claim
that she's dying

until she proves it

Borrowed Time

Reason for referral: no insurance   Of course
Dr. Piper must be paid   So
see the patient   find out
why & how

learn that one day he simply quit
mailing in the premiums   chucked
his job   sold the house
& started driving
to racetracks all over

because he was thirty-four & his father
died at thirty-four & he has
his father's heart he says
so what's the point
& what is there

to persuade him of
except that he's
still here
living
on borrowed time
& that curious medical charity

Grieving

The door opens to light weak as watered sun
She lowers herself as though wounded
into a chair

She has written strange letters   accusing
the doctors   the hospital   *The man in the coffin*
was grim-faced   My husband
was gentle
You listen   helpless   while she chases
her conspiracy tale
The ragged scrap story
whirls round like a dust devil

& slams shut all possible doors
till the room has collapsed
suddenly silent & close as a breathless lung
In her fear she is wearing
the grim face her husband —
No   Never

Her husband was gentle
& vanished impossibly
cleansed of all shadow
like a letter unwriting itself
like a bed sheet unwrinkling

& you are a weak door
she opens & closes again
There is only this wounded light
left to grieve for the body

Did they teach you nothing in school?

Oh certainly:
how to apply
the regulation band-aid
to the immeasurable wound

Hand To Mouth

Old man   at a stroke you toppled
back into infancy
your speech once more the baby mush
of coos & gurgles
Half of you now slumps
useless in the chair
& you cannot be made again
to see it as yours

I who have words can pronounce no miracles
though something your blue eyes find
in my face is wondrous
Your good hand moves to touch it
as I kneel   as if for blessing
or forgiveness   in this forgotten ward
where you wait for some deliverance
or the promised resurrection of the flesh

Never have I been stroked
with such love before   Your worshipful fingers
trace out the whiskered lip
as if preparing to offer up
your gummed-soggy biscuit
in poverty-row communion
hand to mouth

Louise

The nurses say *I'm glad my mother died*
quickly   I'd never go
into one of those homes   Promise me
you'll shoot me if I get like that

Louise is *like that*   Sitting on the commode
she bleats the length of the hallway
Take me to the bathroom   Take me
Take me

They tell her *You're on the toilet   It's OK*
She whimpers *Is this the chair where I can let go?*
Her panic   her desperate dignity
contort her features
Is this it?   Can I let go?
Can I let go?

Yes Louise   This is it
It's all right to let go
Let go now
before hospital policy changes
& nurses patrol the wards with guns in their hands
tracking down their own echoes:
Shoot me if I get like that

Cardiac Arrest

The crash cart stops
at silences   Attempts
to jump-start the heart

The dramatic pause
brings more attention
than the old-timer's had
in years

His loneliness is terminal
Such sudden concern
is a loveless palliation

Like a stuntman on fire
his stardom is measured
in seconds
till he's extinguished

They warned me it can be dizzying to look down
into an open man   They joked
that I should be sure to fall
backward off the stool if I felt faint
But you get used to it

after the shock of that first deliberate
slice into soft pink
fine & clean as a paper cut
when the blood comes quick & alive to the sleeping flesh
& trails the delicate silver blade
down to the tough white backing
which must be scored & stabbed
before it splits like a tight sack

exposing the jelly layer   The fat yields easily
& deep   the slashed capillaries leak blood
into the crevice   So they take what looks like
a dainty soldering iron & sizzle the bright ends
black & neatly shut so the knife can descend
to the stretched red corset of muscle
which is ripped & held open with brute force
that should wake the dead

& you know then
this is no joke   There seems no limit
to the violence they will use
against the wholeness of a man
to save his life   They're sure
they're right to do it

Their gloved hands were in the pit of him past the wrist
& he lost his face for a while
as I was absorbed in his guts
all lumpy wet pink tubes & yellow sacks
with the rubber fingers slipping & digging around
like someone rummaging in a cluttered purse
for a key   I forgot his face
till the knife nicked one wet sack

& a spurt like tobacco juice splattered on my shoe
I saw him again then   eyes shut
his breathing regular
& the stubble of shaved belly hairs
darkening as the antiseptic dried

It was morning outside the room   A winter sun
yawned in the window
A hose slurped up the spill
in the gash of his body
where I could see no answer
to the stranger's open question
only pieces of him being slopped into metal bowls

Empties: A Case of Korsakov's

... doesn't belong here she insists
& he's driving my nurses crazy Day after
unlearnable day   five or six times a shift
the questions: *where's*
the washroom   what sort of place
is this   when
can I go home

The loony bin rejects him out of hand   Relieved
I tell the nurses *Even you*
wouldn't send him there Professional
photographer   chronic drunk
How many empties make twenty years

polaroid backwards?   When he asks
Why am I here? (oh terrible
many-layered question)

I turn it back & watch him
confabulate   He finds   always
the scar below the cheekbone
well-healed decades ago
A diving accident he decides   That must be it

But he feels utterly well now
no trace of the bends —
why don't we discharge him?
To where? Out the window he spies
the North Shore mountains
Out there he answers
Garmisch Partenkirchen

                              Eventually
a group home takes him in   There's talk
of maybe setting up a darkroom
so the man who drank half his life
away can focus   perhaps fix
in its proper country
that range unscalable by medicine
the Alps of perfect forgetting

Saw my first colostomy
while its owner refused to look

He sat wooden on the bedside
as the nurse did things
to a body no longer his

The real expense of my education
was the privacy of others

Watched it all full of book-learnin'
& good intentions:
full of shit

Stroke

Intentions of his limbs   his speech
all haywire   The sun falters in its arc
Stages of the cross   The full weight

of what we're doing here
descends   From upstairs
the watery voices of lovers

quarrelling through tears   I'm no longer
young Sunny Jim from the cereal box
The old man growls at me   alive
in his primitive defences

1. To the Morgue

Nothing sudden happens
No alarm
sounds

There is only
a series of metal doors
& you must
go through them all

Each one clangs heavier
colder
than the last

2. Inventories

A wax-white curtain
partly drawn
A windowless room
tilted
to drain

A list
in chalk:
important body parts

*

The work seems to require:

a hanging grocer's scale
as for weighing vegetables
an assortment of knives & string

as for carving meat

a circular power saw
as for cutting stone

two gentlemen wearing rubber boots
as for wading through mud

3. The Deceased

She had cancer
Then a stroke
left her thoughts wired wrong
She used a child's Magic Slate
when she couldn't find words

I'm too young to be so sick *she said*
Then she wrote on the slate: 34
When the sheet was pulled up
her age disappeared
like magic

4. Specimen Wonders

Dusky grey shifting
to slate-
& steel-blue
to lilac
& plum
to the deep black
redness of wine
the blue blackness
of coal

An evolution of colour
wondrous in its way
but for the fact
that this breathless
lung

came clean & baby pink to the world
& achieved its fatal beauty
with clogged blood

became black-flecked
as though fumbled
wet into ashes

*

Neat & thin: the scalpel

slices a sausage of clotted blood
into dark shining answers

explaining the toes grown cold
& black as a newsboy's fingers

5. The Bound Heart

A body come to grief   Thank God
she vanished before the scalpel
before the shears   before the whining saw
that worked hard at the skull
grinding soft white skull dust
onto the metal bed

Her soul was safe   I clutched the wall
& prayed for mine
as I watched the brain weighed for the record
then handed away to be 'fixed'
while a piece of ribcage was set aside
forlorn as a broken lid

In my own guts I felt the hands
reach in   haul out
more things gone wrong
Then he cut the bound heart free
& it cried
to one who had escaped all measure

6. Hollow

The hollow room
trickles
till somebody chokes off the tap

The silence is very cold
I can hear my heart pounding

In the gutted body
a puddle of blood
like oil

or mud & rain
in an empty
drifting
skiff

7. Outside, After

Crow & white white seabird
yin-yang
in a wheel of flight

lifting my heart
through shadow & light

shadow
& shadow light

35

Dress for Success: A Leaving Poem

Beware of all enterprises that require new clothes
—Thoreau

A nun is a nun
by force of habit
Nurses look naked
in street clothes
Even their envy is uniform
They think I can wear what I like

I am a white
collared
worker
chafed by the fascion fascists
At lunch with my boss
the waiter insisted
I knot something round my neck

Since then this job has been hanging
from a thread

Sudden Infant Death

A too-long day is over & Emergency's just an Exit
to drinks & dinner though
whirling out I recognize
a doctor staggering in

dazed & dishevelled as if struck
by a kind of lightning   Unthinking I assume
the child his patient   then stop
look again at his grief-mad face
& know otherwise

She's limp as the dead Cordelia
in *Lear*'s last act They rush
her from his arms to do
whatever they do
behind the curtains

then they do it a few more times
before sending her by ambulance
to a bigger finer place
that specializes

as if to prove they will
leave no stone unturned
that they will move heaven & earth
for one of their own   And while all this urgent

failure is happening I sit with him
till his nurse wife arrives
then the baby's own doctor
who tries to engage the numb father
in collegial speculation
about *overwhelming*
viral infection

& I am the virtual layman the almost-stranger
useless now as they go away together
to the finer place

so I call the restaurant
where someone who waits to celebrate
my birthday is cursing me
And days later they give me flowers for what
help I'd been & for what I'd said which
couldn't have been anything there'd been
so little to say We'd only waited together
raw with the inconceivable injustice of it
& shut out

of the desperate scurrying futility
knowing they were trying all the magic
he'd already tried & then some
which was nothing finally
because it wasn't enough

And next day on the phone
with the Sudden Infant Death man
who offers parents
the company of misery the bafflement
of experts I spelled out

their names
& professions & recalled
how we'd all sat dumb & staring
at the dreadful emptiness of their trained hands

2. BLACK THREAD

... sad expertise
shadows me even here

In Human Service

In another long blue evening of winter I'm
left behind as the sun slips
down   slides on down & down
to the tropics   You
are among the yellow lights streaming
home as I hold out my arms
now turned to coral   Indifferent
schools of lemon-coloured fish
sweep round & through me   And this is the end
of a working day   a week   a month   a term of
instruction   a course of therapy
in which we have spent our store
of encouraging words   our gestures of
sympathy   exhausted even our desire
for touching hands   This feels like the night
we will burn
down the house just to get warm

Black Thread

To leave behind the silencing
cancers & wander
a geography of voices

To put my ear to the very ground
where the poem is rooted
& hear Homer's oration

To follow him the blind
leading the blind among
islands warm to the touch

back to my own
century & find you on Crete
quoting Elytis

               *   *   *

Among the olive groves & unfaltering sun you ask
for home news   Reluctant
I bring the dark word
of your editor's illness
A tumour in the mouth & she too a poet
Then come the usual questions

Times like these
what wouldn't I give to be someone
else Kirsten or Kate & be asked
how to bathe a baby or frame a house
instead of the inevitable
*What are her chances? Is treatment
hell?* My sad expertise
shadows me even here a black thread
for friends to pull on
unravelling fears

*   *   *

My years at the clinic: too many
voices lost tongues tied
by tumour lips cut
& crookedly closed
dimpled unbeautifully
at the cigarette's perching place
No respecter of persons cancer
& cruel in its ironies blackening
humour with blows to basic functions
defining capacities
      His speech distorted
      by surgery & an ill-fitting denture
      Doktor Freud father of 'the talking cure'
      tells his Parisian visitors
      My prosthesis doesn't speak French
      pries open his teeth with a clothes peg
      to smoke his cigars
      Richard Blessing cursed
      with tumour & graced with
      poetry examines his own brain scan
      & metaphorizes — the convoluted
      lobes are *truly walnuts And Villa-Lobos asked*
      in his last months "Are you composing?"
      replies ruefully No —
      decomposing

However darkened poetry & song
endure To the end even beyond Let us remember this
we who are sound

    *   *   *

Weeks later I sail off into Eco's
essays hike the novels of Dürrenmatt
take the night train to the heart
of Machado's poems   I'm transported
by national voices the journey's

a run-on sentence in many languages
I miss the glottochronology but not the root
-words the common threads:
speranza esperanza espoir ...
I send you a bright postcard
& *sotto voce* a prayer
between the lines:

Let cancer never translate her
into silence   How would we know
we've come home
without her voice?

Hot-house Babies

The hot-house babies sing themselves
lullabies with irregular rhythms
Not ready yet
is the only lyric they know

Like kites at the end of their tether   they soon
must fall into the world
or sail away forever out of sight

We wonder how to hold them
when they are here & not quite here
So frail & wizened   they've managed a miracle
travelling this far   Unlanded immigrants
hung up for weeks in customs   they are
suspect refugees   illegal
aliens

We tell ourselves we will love them
over the threshold
into existence   Their tiny
troubled footprints
hesitate

TB Sanatorium

You arrive for the conference
& realize what the building used to be
You go in   clutching manila folders
your brown bag lunch   How many years
since there has been no sound
you wonder

East wing   west wing   upper & lower levels
the miles of corridors stripped echoless
of wheeled beds trundled from rooms
to balconies   You imagine
the patients draining
their lungs & faces in the sun

From room to spartan room
you search out a door with speech
behind it   You cough
are answered by coughs

And it grips you
You run from the air that's been trapped
in brown bags & passed through the keyholes
You are outside again   breathing
as deep as you can
till it hurts

Wishbone

In the schoolyard of Our Lady
of Perpetual Help
his strange brace catches
the winter light

He is dancing his jig
as evidence
in a circle of unmaimed friends
See him straddle
the heavy memento
See him laughing
away the cross

that holds his legs
open   making his bones
a wishbone
making his dance
the wishbone dance

Bread and Death

We were in the car   ready
to go to the zoo
My dad went back in the house
to get bread for the animals ...

The way Ross told it
with the climax enigmatically offstage
turned it into a parable
whose meaning I couldn't quite catch
The age we were then   the world was all
suggestion   a big suit we'd never grow into
a father's trick

with coins or cards   And now
this sinister link between animals
& death   Or bread & death   And whose
risky idea was it anyway?   Deep
consequences for even the smallest choices
made at the last minute
The very last

Cowboy

25   maybe
younger   *an Indian cowboy*
in the rodeo

Had to hang on to break
eight seconds   Broke
his back instead

Split-second life-change
Fate's horse-laugh at young male pride
Now he wrangles
a wheelchair   dangles
wasted legs between parallel bars
while the big-city therapist
spurs him on

In ideal circumstances, an ideal donor — a young, otherwise-healthy
MVA victim — can provide body materials to 40 or 50 recipients
—overheard at Teaching Rounds

Walking home from work as an ambulance comes
wailing round the curve   Cyclist

smudged out
between gravel truck & bus

Body materials on offer:
bone   skin   etcetera
50 recipients?
20?
Any takers?

Precious Groceries

We assume darkness inside the body
that the light goes out when the door is closed
By what right

do we abandon each other
instead of forever the way we were as children
clutched to the breast with a strong arm —
oh precious groceries! How wrong

to fall   to lie in the melting snow
split open like a paper sack
with the light & all the hopeful
red rhythm spilling out

Giving Blood, Making a Fist

... what else is there to think about
except that one day blood may call us
together — four brothers   alike &
distant as the corners of a room
We'll be forced to trust
strangers to say who is most
compatible   & who most dangerous
One of us will lie
pale on the pillow   weakening
like headlights burning through the day
Someone will whisper *marrow*
or *kidney*   & the chains of
brotherhood will tense in rescue

My Father's Heart

Keeps it in his tool box   Believes
it's safer there   Who am I
to suggest otherwise after his brother & sister
pulled over to the shoulder of their lives
& died young   clutching
the fabric of the everyday?   Why
encourage him to surrender

it to the doctors   ticket-takers
of the operating theatre or the grave
who he fears will tear it in half smile
& say *Go right in*?   I want to whisper
Wrong currency   but what else does he have
what else would their power accept?
He's not one of those persons of privilege
eager to have theirs surgically removed
to create a deeper pocket for their cash   No

he says a used one is better
than nothing   Even a broken one
works right enough in its fashion   The stairway
of argument ends in mid-air   language hesitates
turns   descends again bewildered   Perhaps   after all
he knows his own heart best   I've seen it
only once   It had nail holes in it

3. INFORMATION AND SPECIAL INSTRUCTIONS

... as though you were
moving

Information and Special Instructions

a found poem

the following is presented so you may understand
a long drawn out condition
recovery often slow

cooperate with us
injections are practically painless
should be no reaction of any kind
important to control certain
contributory factors
e.g. emotional disturbances

      *   *   *

guessing has little place in the practice of medicine

we find it necessary
to make our own
even if previously done

most patients who follow orders are
benefited we often inspect a patient's
home to see if instructions are carried out

      *   *   *

no two cases alike certain
rules may be laid down
      avoid anything which causes an attack
      whisk-brooms are pernicious
      rubber bedding advised
      keep away from people with "colds"
      avoid over-exertion
      live moderately keep your appointments
      move out of the home
      until the odour is gone

*　　*　　*

keep the windows shut
if you go away you may suffer
intensely
do not be misled
permanent relief is rare

*　　*　　*

because of intimate contact
impossible for your physician
involving the face
neck   bends of the elbows and knees

if you get any ideas
write them down

they will not be forgotten

if there is anything
telephone
or write

remember

what we are doing now is
to prevent worse
trouble in the future

*　　*　　*

swellings are usually larger
an eyelid the tongue or a lip
a burning feeling
sometimes prolonged
search for the cause
is necessary

        *   *   *

most people cannot control their
daylight hours   the bedroom
cleaned daily   a thorough cleaning
once a week   while the directions may seem
difficult experience
plus habit will make them
simple well worth the effort
        several layers of cheesecloth some other
        adequate material
        the room completely emptied
        just as though you were
        moving
        every inch of exposed or hidden
        surface spic and span
        only one bed preferably a simple
        iron bed
        do not use blankets
        do not have any stuffed toys
        a wooden chair which has been scrubbed
        may be used   plain light curtains
        washed once a week
        the room should contain
        a minimum
        air thoroughly
        then close the door and windows

        *   *   *

best results can usually be obtained
in the young   many parents are
too easy-going   children "potential"
individuals hence must be watched
most carefully from the day they are born
their contact with ordinary
substance closely scrutinized
cats dogs and "fuzzy" toys
should be kept away
in picking the child up do not allow
his skin to come in contact
with wool or
silk or
furs

               *   *   *

          do not have hobbies
          do not wear any pure silk
          avoid animals and birds none
          should be admitted
          get rid of any you have
          do not go into barns or stables
          do not play in tall grasses
          it is very important
          almost certainly

4. THE CUT DAY

... to feel the edge

Living with Cancer

The new patient is appalled at the gallows
humour before the meeting starts
Loose talk about death

has spooked him driven him
to the edge

of our circle where he whispers to his wife
about leaving early

Newly hired I'm here to observe the human
chemistry as the group administers a dose
of distilled experience Cancer
is alive in the room yet the laughing presence

of ten- & twelve-year veterans
confounds the man's fear

When I started work someone issued me
a daybook Religiously I snip a corner
off each clean page as it comes

to be always in the present to feel the edge
of the cut day against my thumb & know I am right
where I belong
                        Tomorrow we will spread
out in a bigger building my office
one cell in a growing cancer

clinic Like the stranger tonight I'm new
to this disease but as a comfort
the old hands assure me
we will soon be
well acquainted

Between tears
during Living with Cancer
they'd hear sometimes the fright-squeal of pigs

experimental subjects
wheeled in under cover of night

Tearing Down

Tears have rusted the locks   warped the tiles
Floors have buckled under the weight of ghosts
Nothing scours us so clean as destruction
Punctured   the rooms exhale a sour breath

We yearn to be shiny & new   to be feeding dead patients
into computer memory   free at last
of the terrible burden their paper names became
ever increasing   crowding the living out

And now we are full of our powers   aggressively curious
proud & fiercely armed   We call it science
call it fighting fire with fire   an affirmation
a wrecker's ball smashing like a dead fist against the stones

The Night Man

What do I know about grieving?   Not as much
as the night man   who washes again the face
of the hospital moon

clanging his metal bucket
down the corridors of loss
Dirty water sloshes over the lip

It takes a while to die   The soon-to-be widow
switches off thought with TV   lets her heart
glaze over   Not even thirty & already caught
in a Movie-Disease-of-the-Week   Immersed
in the soaps   she learns gestures
she'll need later on

At the gravesite we are clumsy & green
together   our hands hold the death
& each other badly   Confused
by this cold passion   I ache to know
what the night man knows
as she buries
her tear-stained face
in the murky water of my breast

Prosthetics

He gives me eyes
to stare back at

hands me a nipple
he made himself

He admits that sometimes
his people are disappointed

He has to remind them
gently
he isn't God

though he's laboured longer
on the blues of an iris
or an ear's
curled
mystery

The spare parts man
does brave work

but he shies away
from my praise

When he gives me his hand
it's warm
& his smile is genuine

Place gun firmly in the mouth   not
shaking at your temple

lest Prosthetics be forced to devise another
pink mask with painted eyes
to cover the bullet-carved hollow
of blind living flesh

The Coming of Spring

From Port-of-Spain
to the snow
he has come to burned

clean with radiation
rescued by poisons
The hollows of his eyes
are deep pools of faith
Chin whiskers
like fine black grass
sprout hopefully

His words have a soft
island music   *My country*
he whispers
is a beautiful place
so very beautiful
They drain his blood
for evidence   Under the microscope
an aerial photo of islands
Malignant invasion

Against the white pillow
his dark gleaming skull
is sculpted
smooth   imperceptibly
closer to final perfection
Into his ears   the Walkman is chanting
Koran: *In the name of Allah*
the compassionate
the merciful

Chances Are

Remember how *I love you*
sounded when my voice was all gravel & smoke?
Rougher than a stretch of dirt road in summer   Soon
it was less than a croak just a dry
whisper like dust settling after
the car's gone by   I told you then
Tenderness is hard

Before they cut out the voice
box   a pretty girl came by
with a book of comforting
words   It had sketches
of a man & woman embracing   & it said
if you loved me before
chances are you would love me
again   Words   it seems   are just vibrating air

given pretty shape in a mouth   Perhaps I can learn
to burp *I love you* into your ear   If not
I can buy a machine
that vibrates love
& rage & singing
into one robotic monotone of loss

On Reading Poems by Women with Breast Cancer

... I think of my colleague Lis   who shows women
to her gentle office where they're entitled to their tears
& one free prosthesis   *I can't promise*
a perfect match she says *but*
no two are identical anyway   She might be describing
the women — no two the same
in their anger   their grief   the new tenderness they feel
at the lost flesh   They rummage among fakes
for one that will have to do   There are too many

& not enough   Like metaphors
of Amazons & heartbreak   they are soon
shop-worn & sad   In dreams that childhood ghost
Susie Homemaker   mender of all torn things
proffers the missing breast to be sewn back on
At last   the balancing
weight & shape   the familiar
warmth of the real   But waking   a woman
of blood & bone takes into her hands
the unequal halves of her life

Ron and Don

Called to your dying twin   you will not
stay   Duty
pity can compel
only so much   I do
a double take coming out of his room
seeing him in you   fleshed out
like a second chance

You go in   talk perhaps 10 minutes
then you're back   saying
he wants sleep & you want
lunch   You're satisfied
with one glance in the distorted mirror
It's enough — one terrible glimpse
of how you may end

But an instant later   he's yelling
Where's my brother?   protesting
he only closed his eyes for a moment
You turn   mouth twitching the twitch
his mouth makes
under stress   The look you wear
says *What does he want from me?*

Later   you wonder aloud who'll tie up his affairs
wanting someone   anyone but yourself
to get things done   *I don't know his life
out here   don't know his friends
We haven't been close ...*   And can't bear to be
close now   Close as the two halves of
a cancer cell dividing   Close as
the rhymed syllables of your names

Flight Paths

1.

Waiting his turn to lie exposed
beneath the fearsome machines
he explains to me the truth
about cancer-and-magnetism

suggested by something he saw
in a Lauren Bacall movie   though poleaxed

by her beauty he stumbles
on the title   *She was flying*
in a plane   The compass
went suddenly haywire   It's easily
the morning's most dizzying theory

2.

With chemo burning his veins the lymphoma patient
tells how the Hindenburg fire
destroyed all hope

of commercial dirigible use   Unfairly
since the death toll no worse
than a modern airline crash   Eloquent

even poetic he describes their gentle nature
pictures them hovering low licking
poisoned waters clean

That night the great ship enters my dreams
pale & soundless
floating huge in the night sky:

submerged Beluga

slow elongated moon

sex organ
bobbing in bathwater

white elephant
led on a string by a child

Survivors

1. The Sister

In the bald fact of his death at 20
she confronts the underside
of the grand design: a mare's nest
of fine black threads   a circuit apparently
hard-wired for static   The whispers

of well-intentioned friends offer her
all the reassurance of a dry broom
sweeping it under the rug   *And yet* she thinks

perhaps they're right — that by and by
a meaning may emerge   I've known scars
to assume the shapes of letters
seen cracks in the wall
slowly become a face

But for now   there is only bafflement
& an undiminishing ache
as night after night
the angel of irrational numbers
visits   Picking the lock
of her heart   he steals
into her dreams   Through the hollow hours
she weeps beneath the shelter
of his broken wings

2. The Mother

Well & whole   she was a part
of his slow blue dying
She prayed & wept   her heart
following him to the end
of the earth for a cure   Why
should miracles always be distant
something so different from where
& who we are?   She remembers
him coming back   after
the miracle had failed
wearing a nautical flag on his chest
that warned: *Stay away! I'm on fire*
and have dangerous cargo on board
She flung her arms around that fire
crushed it to her
& she is burning still
though he is gone

Her galloping cancer a godsend
to the devoted husband
who turned up faithfully to renew her prescriptions

She'd been dead for weeks before Pharmacy
finally caught on   While pain ate her up
& after
he stayed high on the morphine
sold the rest on the street for a quick buck

Miss B's Virus

Pulled back & knotted
her hair's the white-yellow of
broken dentures   Flattered at first
to be recognized & addressed
she seeks me out later
& whispers her wish

to be only *Miss B.* in future
& never accept
the bad name this place gives her
I always avoided cancer
patients — thought it might be
a virus   Now she fears
a similar shunning
declines the offered ride

unless an unmarked car will wait
somewhere the neighbours won't see
& the drivers stop insisting on her name

for their computer   She talks
hackers & viruses says
the pharmacy computer killed a patient
overdosing his morphine   *They still*

don't know   It could be a virus
Sipping shallow breaths she departs
this tainted air   bird-like
wasted away to a spinster initial

Dust/Jacket

Circles of testing   as with any found pen
He keeps coming around   to linger
among the living   *His admirers*
have had his inimitable
book of recollections   He draws out
the most meaningless
conversations

It is hard
It is hard to think   Circles
of testing   as with any found pen
The poems have been very carefully
arranged to form a whole   Takes off
the jacket with the gold braid
Shows us his medal   It is hard
to linger among the living   *To have them as a book*
enhances each and every one

The cruel notion of his own death
of turning to dust   keeps
coming round   as with any found pen
The living: it is hard to think of them
Among the living   it is hard to form a whole

He draws out the most
meaningless conversations   Takes off the jacket
with the gold braid turning to dust   Shows us
his medal   his own death   testing
admirers   *It is hard to think of them*
out of context   He keeps coming round
very carefully arranged   The jacket
His medal   Inimitable
recollections   Living
enhances
each & every one

He said back home young docs earned
a flat fee for pronouncing death
No cheques   Easy
money   Everyone knew it as
ash cash

The Book of the Dead

Housekeeping proves that death
is always with us   Every month at the clinic
a list comes round & I'm expected to prune from my files
the names that are mine: Leo Shirley
Alfred Enid Stan ...

Most of us say we hate this part
when ASSISTANT GRIM REAPER becomes
our new job title I try to see it instead as
a kind of training a chance to develop
my latent angelic nature

I confess I haven't the heart
to use the trashcan   Month after month
I ferry these souls to a big black binder I call
the Book of the Dead   There they live
alongside their alphabetical neighbours
in the new development   It helps them
—& me — not to feel so suddenly lost

If I'm in this work much longer I'll need
Volume II   One day we will all be forgotten
so I know I'm just stalling for time   But when I go
I plan to take The Book with me
to bring to God's notice the lives
of his suffering people   Fiercely
exasperating people some of them
who I think of now

with great fondness *These are my dead*
I say to myself conscious of a strange
possessiveness Ironic since the truth of it is
that I am the one possessed —
by their irascible voices
reciting to me the litany of their troubles
garrulous to the end & loathe to leave

Taking Your Lumps
for Cora

The 97-year-old you attend
stares unrepentant at your
increasingly misshapen face

then blurts out *Are you married?*
You guess where this is leading

*You bring that boyfriend in then
I'll straighten him out   What's
his name?*   The feisty old dame
weighs less than her years
but would rise indignant

from her wheelchair to your defence
His name?   *Mel* you're tempted to say
"Malignant" Mel

Anoma   Foreign
to her no doubt   Not many become intimate
with such a batterer   Doctors
offer restraining orders   nothing

divorces you for good   there's no shelter
you can run to   Except perhaps
laughter —

ours
your own — as you live again
the rich moment
here in a circle of friends
who've acquired in these last months
a taste for such black humour

From the monitor it shines
azure through the dark
a true revelation inviting

our unscientific ooohs & aaahs
It's abstract art ...
... so pretty!
... tile your bathroom in large cell lymphoma?
Rapt while the patient shivers
in the next room we forget
a moment what malignancy means

give in
to a different order of understanding
even as patients sometimes step outside
their panic   (Richard

Blessing the poet
looked up at CTs
of his tumorous brain
thinking Hemispheres — yes
they really do look like walnuts!)

Our pathologist fixes his van Gogh eye
to the 'scope & asks us to appreciate
the starry sky appearance   *There is a heaven —*

he seems to be saying — swirling above
& within us

a great wheel

& in it the beautiful
seeds of our own destruction

The Book of the Living
for William

Dead-easy to love the ones
who are fixed
in memory   It's the living —
to care for you is to
lean out heart exposed
into the fickle winds of chance

Remembering you to your doctor
I say you sound well & happy
Yes he says *I think*
we cured him

Cured — the word rings a long time
in his wake its pure confidence still
something scarcely dared   My heart sings
a small prayer for you bends to drink
this water from another's hands

The dead visit often the living
hardly ever save for
the shadow people parolees
who return for months & years never sure
if they've violated some minor condition
& will be snatched again

into custody   They
polaroid slowly back into life
taking on definition & colour
as check-up intervals lengthen
& they begin to see themselves
again   the sweet needles
of feeling return
as to a blood-starved limb   Ruefully
they examine

before & after photographs recognize
survivors scarred in mind & body
who know too much
to ever take sunrise for granted   They dream of cure

like an unconditional pardon
If it comes most take it & run
without looking back   But you
relive it all: the car crash
that killed your father-in-law
days before cancer

blindsided you   how from weathered Shuswap totems
that bodied kinship to raven & orca
you found yourself tethered to a
hope-slim IV pole   how we'd find you
face to the wall could coax from you
only whispers

Of the small steps by which we
walked you back to the world the chart records
only professional generalities: *Patient seen
for support. Mood improving* Now
in the Bosch painting of your life
Death is once more

a minor figure amid children lawnmowers
& bingo In my book of the living
the book of joy you are
page one

A Hand on the Belly

I'm learning to breathe she tells us
which sounds like more proof
should we need it
of how some events undo
everything obliging us to start over
from the beginning

                    Staff pregnancies are
a treat at the cancer clinic We
make much of that first swelling
which is not — thank God —
is *not* an evil omen   Comparing
symptoms the vets reassure the first timers
That's normal Sure That's normal
Really it is

                    This is growth with
order for once with a plan Not that other
irregular madness all around us Every day
we speak softly to people deafened by the sound
of the cancer ticking louder & louder inside them
They're still praying someone will rush in
with the right x-rays while along the hall
resplendently inflated with health & optimism
another white bloom of fruitfulness
floats by

                    In the agony of waiting
rooms the patients divide themselves
into silent camps of the envious the bitter
& the momentarily cheered who wonder if it would help
to stretch out a hand & lay it against that perfect
utterly fleshy vessel of hope
to feel the kick   to take up
the heat of life

Medicine

I have travelled in cities of the East & held out
my paper token   The black-suited subway man bites
a neat piece of it with his metal punch & in between
passengers his *tic tic tic* continues   The tiny jaws continue
tic tic tic   In Seoul's medicine shops are glass bottles
where herbalists display unusual growths
of ginseng shaped like people   All this beneath the city —
trains worm their way through cold tunnels
& the ginseng sellers advise on the endless complaints
of middle-age   while at produce stalls I hear
the nervous *tic tic tic* of the vendor's trimming shears

And I have travelled in cities of the West where radioactive cobalt
must be replaced in the machines before reaching its half-life
A patient gingerly fingers the bulge of his cancer & calculates
whether he's too young to die or too old to be tortured
on the slim chance of cure   No one is sure   Even the doctor
speaks as if ticking down
a list of well-practised evasions   Experience tells him
that truth is too potent & must be replaced
with half-truth   as a dose of radiation is dispensed
in fractions   although hope too is an old & unusual growth
often strong as the roots of stones   & human-shaped

EPILOGUE

The Soul Departs

When the soul departs it leaves behind
the fork & knife
of this life

the pipe & slippers
coins & clocks
all instruments of measure

Cut loose from distinction it floats
wavering
up from an ocean's depth
shedding blues & greens
& the heart's firm purpose
to breach in a new element

Of which there is something familiar
but more shining
Which requires it seems
another way of breathing

Certain mountains were like this in life
& certain dreams
& certain griefs

& yet this is different
from all that went before

What were once the mortal eyes have been washed
the clockwork that ticked in the skull
opens now like a rose *Yes?* says the soul timidly
Yes? Yes?

The soul arriving
shakes like a slackened sail
not sure not yet quite sure
how much it misses the body

Notes

Worker Classification: Material Handler — 'Material Handler' was the designation given by Canada Manpower, as it was then called, to unskilled warehouse labourers.

Empties: A Case of Korsakov's — Korsakov's Syndrome is a confusional state, especially as to recent events, due to brain injury or toxic causes such as chronic alcoholism.

Garmisch-Partenkirchen is a winter resort at the foot of the highest peak in Germany.

Black Thread — Canadian poet, fiction writer and editor Bronwen Wallace died of oral cancer in 1989.

Sigmund Freud was diagnosed with oral cancer in 1923; he underwent numerous treatments over many years, and died of his disease in 1939. His remark "My prosthesis doesn't speak French" is quoted in *The Life and Work of Sigmund Freud* by Ernest Jones.

Richard Blessing was a Seattle writer who documented his response to his cancer diagnosis and treatment in his collection *Poems and Stories*. He died in 1983.

Brazilian composer Heitor Villa-Lobos was diagnosed with bladder cancer in 1948. Treated surgically, he was well for 11 years, but died of complications in 1959. His answer to the question "Are you composing?" is quoted in the CBC Radio documentary, *The Indian in the Tuxedo*.

Hot House Babies — Parents of infants who die in the Neo-natal ICU often want tangible mementoes of their child's brief life. Along with the child's hospital ID bracelet, social workers sometimes provide a set of the baby's footprints.

Cowboy — 'He's an Indian Cowboy in the Rodeo' is a song by Buffy Sainte-Marie.

Dust/Jacket — The italicized passages come from the dust jacket of W.S. Merwin's *Opening the Hand*.

Path. Review — CT, or, more fully, CAT, is an acronym for Computerized Axial Tomography, a form of diagnostic imaging comparable to an X-ray.

The Soul Departs — This poem is inspired by the Paul Klee painting of the same name.